My
Rainbow
Poetry
Rosanne Barca

To order additional copies of this book, contact:
Proisle publishing Services LLC
1177 6th Ave 5th Floor
New York, NY 10036, USA
Phone: (+1 347-922-3779)
info@proislepublishing.com

PROISLE PUBLISHING

My Rainbow Poetry

This book of poems and photography is dedicated to my family:

Rosemarie and Frank, my parents: for giving me life, love, guidance, support, love of sport, travel, adventure and my sister Maria

Maria, my sister: for giving me love, support and my two nephews: Robert and David

Aunt Fannie and Uncle Sam, my Godparents: for giving me love, religion, support, music, fun and my cousin Annette

Uncle Louis and Aunt Sue: for giving me love, support, laughter, great food and my two cousins: Sam and Jeff

Aunt Rose: for giving me love, support, Palm Sunday dinners, travel and love of the arts

I am so thankful to my entire family and all my friends who have shared in so many wonderful memories.

Love and peace to all,

Rosanne Barca

Table Of Contents

Carefree Love

Love come down and smile on me
once it did and it was clear
the only thing in life that mattered.

I miss the days of carefree love.

Wanting to feel your sweet touch
thinking of how it used to be
smiling inside because I was full.

I miss the days of carefree love.

Hoping to find again someday
that feeling that I thought would never leave
in my heart, a part of you is there.

I still miss the days of carefree love.

Love Is King

Wow you're here
by my side

I'm so happy
I can fly

Hold my hand
I need to know

You feel the same
feel all aglow

not just above
but below

Yes I want you
let me take you now

Share this moment
and be proud

Love is everything
Love is king

Kiss me over
and over again

Stay with me
til wakening

so we can smile
and be happy

cause love is king
love is everything

The Shoreline

It's been a long drive
eight hours or more
to the outer banks
from the jersey shore

I love it here
and I love it there
the ocean is magic
so much beauty to share

The shoreline is long
the east coast is varied
what a perfect place
to decide to get married

it's one place on earth
that makes you feel
so many feelings
that keep you real

Come What May

Its been seven years maybe eight
since our last date

some things have changed
everythings rearranged

lets make amends
and be friends

for the better you say
come what may

heres my number
remember our first summer

let the good times roll
my heart you stole

love with every beat
until liquors defeat

Its been seven years maybe eight
since our last date

I pick up the phone
hear a dial tone

my fingers fumble
dialing your number

I hear your hello
lets take it slow

one day at a time
is my favorite line

conversing went on
and on and on

like time stood still
there's no ill will

for the better you say
come what may

Time

time to relax
time to think
time to decide
time to ink

it's been a while
for clarity to take hold
life's been so cloudy
its time to be bold

to take hold of the reins
thats been holding you down
yell let's get on with it
start pounding the ground

time never waits
life is too short
stop tempting fate
call your cohort

stop being afraid
of what may not come
go after your destiny
run Forest run

I Hope You Find What You're Looking For

I hope you find what you're looking for
who knows what's behind that door
must open it up to explore
hope to find what you're looking for

Did you find what you're looking for
was it right there behind that door
did you open it up and get what you want
or do you keep on wanting more

do you keep on wanting more
do you keep on wanting more
I hope you find what you're looking for
I hope you find what you're looking for

True Friends

true friends
know who they are
they're in your heart
whether near or far

true friends
know who they are
speak with them often
they're in your memoirs

true friends
know who they are
nourish each other
they're you're costar

true friends
know who they are
make music together
and become rockstars

true friends
know who they are
let live laugh and love
be your North star

true friends
know who they are
unconditionally love you
and accept who you are

true friends
I know who you are
I love you and thank you
my rocks and my stars

Like Minds

Is it me or you, its hard to tell
we think along the same lines

its refreshing knowing
we're not alone anymore

there are others out there
waiting to be reached

a lifeline of kindred souls
another voice is heard

keep on speaking
I love listening to you

Your way with words
clarifies my thoughts

verifies my feelings
my life is valid

I am not alone
I am among the living

constantly learning
and not fearing

to be myself
at peace in my skin

thanks to you
my new found friend

The Game

Its either the NY Yankees
or the NY Mets
both baseball teams
if you can't guess

Win win is what
they try to do
to get the best record
to impress me and you

Going to the ballpark
is always great fun
sitting on the edge of your seat
hoping for a home run

A really great game
can be a slugfest or pitchers duel
it depends on the lineup
that the managers rule

When its time for lunch
it's a ballpark frank
some peanuts and Cracker Jack
almost break the bank

It's the top of the ninth
the home teams ahead
three more outs
no more to be said

So lets root for the home team
as the old song goes
everyone's standing
up on their toes

Now it's one out to go
and the ump calls strike three
the stadium is rockin
fans shoutin' with glee

The game may be over
but only for today
cause tomorrow
they're scheduled to play in LA

Disappointed Again

never to refrain
nor to abstain
only to remain
disappointed again

deep in the vein
is the dark pain
only to remain
disappointed again

burnt is the brain
tired and insane
only to remain
disappointed again

ran to the train
in the fast lane
only to remain
disappointed again

drank champagne
on an airplane
only to remain
disappointed again

vacationed in Spain
returned to Maine
only to remain
disappointed again

tried in vain
to break the chain
only to remain
disappointed again

by the constant strain
of life's big drain
only to remain
disappointed again

I Am Worthy

fear shall not beat me
why is it so halting
I try to go forward
yet I am defaulting

so onward and upward
one step at a time
I climb up that mountain
and continue to find

is it the unknown
unfamiliar territory to sow
how will I react
how will I grow

if I don't move ahead
no change will occur
so I keep on moving
and let my life soar

will tomorrow be better
can I still move ahead
only I can decide
to emerge from my bed

time is telling
I keep taking a stand
now I fly with the eagles
with success in my hands

only I can decide
to move ahead
for I am worthy
I have said

Flights Delayed

Flights delayed
rain go away
hope to depart
sometime today

Someone is waiting
for me to come
vacation plans
have just begun

Clouds are lifting
the sky clears
my plane's on time
have no fear

I will arrive
without a hitch
find my way
make my niche

The party is
about to start
it's time to board
my plane departs

A Portrait

a thought to pen
awaiting creation
as I pose for you

your brush strokes
linseed oil and paint
my portrait being born

watching you create
squinting to see
shadows on my face

a twinkle in your eye
a smile on your face
stress is all erased

you are flowing
with rainbow colors
flying from your brush

once a blank canvas
now captures my essence
behold a masterpiece

Allergies Allergies

voice is hoarse
nose is runny
spring is here
it's not funny

eyes are red
burning itching
nose will not
stop its sneezing

leaves sprouting
trees blooming
throat so sore
from much coughing

take a pill
for some relief
nose spray too
but it's so brief

I love spring
but it has its price
allergies allergies
to be precise

Stop Before You Start

You've got to stop the violence
to give peace a chance
You've got to start to love
what happened to romance

You've got to stop the hate
cause hate will only kill
You've got to start to love
and spread some good will

You have to stop the war
to start to free your mind
You have to stop the confusion
to start your mind to unwind

You've got to stop the killing
and start to love one another
You've got to stop the hatred
start to love each sister and brother

You've got to stop and think
to start all the healing
You've got to stop tearing down
to start all the building

You've got to stop it now
and turn it all around
You've got to start it now
to be strong and be sound

You've got to stop the hate
before it's just too late
You've got to start to love
cause it's our world at stake

You have to stop the hate
before you can begin
to start to give love
to all God's children

Olympic Superstar

Prepare to
run jump dance
pose and
hold that stance

Slowly approach
jump flip dive
with little splash
you may survive

But there are others
wanting the same
so there's no time
to be tame

So you give it all
and hope your best
will place you on top
above all the rest

first second third
gold silver bronze
if not now
four years to wait on

To think to train
to do it over
again
and again

To prepare for the moment
of fame and glory
all must be perfect
to end the story

of how you became
an Olympic superstar
representing a country
from near or afar

as your medal rests
upon your chest
you have valid proof
you're among the best

Peace To All

Peace begins with me
I extend my hand to you
to share and to see
what one hand can do

Please pass on your hand
to someone new
spread through the land
not just to a few

That peace is to share
with one another
so show you care
to every sister and brother

Hand by hand
from sea to sea
throughout the land
from you to me

So make a difference
one at a time
always reference
love and be kind

As the words of love and peace
spread to one and all
hate will ease
walls will fall

So don't forget
to extend your hand
and have no regret
to take a stand

As the world becomes
a better place
hatred succumbs
love wins the race

The world can live
hand in hand
as we forgive
peace commands

I love You

I love you
I miss you
I so much
want to kiss you

Feel our lips touching
tongues dancing
hot breath teasing
our bodies quivering
with delight

on a moon lit night
or in a sunny daylight
I long to touch you
and please you
can't wait to see you
tonight

Life Is Short

Life is short
is what I always heard
now I can confirm
those very words

I am now 45
and time flies right on by
just like they said
in a blink of an eye

It was just the holidays
and tomorrow it will be May
where did those 4 months go
it went so fast I just don't know

Time and time again
remember this my friend
always live for today
don't wait for a holiday

To share your time
or spend your last dime
cause all your loved ones
will get your funds

In the end
I hope its love you send
when you look back
to those words on the plaque

That say life is short
don't be a worrywort
and laugh out loud
thinking aloud

How time flew by
in a blink of an eye
the holidays are cast
and another years past

Hurricane Katrina

In sixty nine it was Camille
that ravaged the gulf shore
in 2005 Katrina did
much more as a category four

water water everywhere
for as far as you could see
destruction and devastation
from the rivers to the sea

I couldn't believe my eyes
but it was right in front of me
begging and crying loudly
for help on my TV

In homeland America
a great disaster unveiled
again the U.S. comes together
and once again we'll prevail

through the chaos and confusion
heros rose and fell
but for days on end the people
thought they were in pure hell

Donations were received
from near and abroad
we all couldn't believe it
and we were totally floored

it will take many months
maybe years to rebuild
before the waterfronts
and streets are all healed

but what about the people
where will they all be
under a great steeple
holding a skeleton key

waiting patiently to learn
around and in the Astrodome
when they can return
to a place once called home

I Miss You

its two weeks
since I saw you last
seems much longer
than the time that past

a lot has happened
I want to discuss
why won't you call
have I lost your trust

I love you
is what I want to say
but I'm afraid
that will keep you away

its only a friend
that you're looking for
I thought the same
but I feel so much more

I backed away
to avoid the hurt
its only the pain
I try to avert

now its your turn
for needed space
I'm patiently waiting
for your warm embrace

to pick up
where we left off
God I'm
such a jerkoff

the last thing I wanted
was to ever hurt you
I'm so very sorry
if I made you blue

another days gone
and I miss you

Wondering

Waking as the sun rises
Wondering when
When will I see you again

Listening to the music on the radio
Wondering when
When will I see you again

Staring at the phone
Wondering when
When will we speak again

Dining alone
Wondering when
When will I see you again

Watching the sunset
Wondering when
When will I see you again

Gazing at the stars
Wondering when
When will I see you again

Waiting day after day
Wondering when
When will this longing end

Rock On

Music is another love of mine
I go to many concerts
Always a great time.

To really rock
You need
Guitars, drums and bass.

Just add
some lyrics
To state your case.

Another story, another tune
Just listen to the music
And you too can croon.

An Art Form

It starts with a pattern
That gets cut up
Then pick the colors
That fill your cup

The glass it is shiny
With much allure
The cuts are all different
Flux and solder secure

What will it be
This puzzle of glass
It will be known
When the last piece is cast

Its time to clean
With soap and water
To remove any flux
And beads of solder

Be it patina or polish
Its up to your eye
To antique or leave silver
To make the buyer sigh

Your work its complete
You did your best
You can now call yourself
A stained glass artist

God Took You Home

So it is said
let it be
but how can I
watch it ending

to see you there
in such pain
its so hard
but I remain

I don't want to
leave you alone
I must stay
to keep you strong

I hold your hand
as you cry out
I'm right here
I say out loud

The tears they roll
down my face
why so much pain
do you have to face

I never thought
it would end this way
but in my heart
you will always stay

You have taught me much
throughout my days
I will never forget
as I keep the faith

that as long as I live
always share my love
and always forgive
like the Lord above

for true peace in your heart
you must believe
that God is by your side
and will never leave

and that is how I know
that as you left this life
God was by your side
as you headed toward the light

That was my comfort
to know you were not alone
and in my sorrow
God took you home

But I believe
we will meet again
someday not too soon
much more work to tend

Now you're an angel
to guard and guide
forever more I pray
please be by my side

Change

change is constant
I've always heard
but not for some
they're like a jailbird

confined and restricted
by their recurring thoughts
seems hard to even breathe
like lungs with bloodclots

brain waves are the same
weaving up and down
seems just like a moving
merry go round

why can't you change
like most everyone else
I don't understand it
can't you feel the pulse

I guess if you knew better
you would surely try
but I was totally wrong
cause you choose to die

drowning in those thoughts
wishing would set you free
when all they brought you
was heartache and misery

it's sad to see a life
just waste away
when there's so much more
to discover each day

change is constant
that much is true
and change is a choice
that's up to you.

I Am

its been a while
since i've written
dont know why
hope i'm forgiven

life has been
ebb and flow
so many changes
and things let go

change is good
for the soul
listening carefully
to the bowls

sounds are ringing
clear as a bell
feelings clearing
all going well

moving forward
one step at a time
keeping life's momentum
in three quarter time

my life is a song
singing loud and clear
being proud and strong
having no fear

for i am who i am
and no one else
as i am beautiful
just being myself

Hello Valentine

hello valentine
will you be mine

we are so different
yet the same

both wanting love
but will refrain

too afraid
to hurt the other

cause were more like sisters
than like lovers

yes that love
is hard to find

so much easier
in my mind

where there I can hold you
without regret

and kiss you
until content

if only this love
was felt by you too

until that day
this dream won't come

oh sweet valentine
I wish you were mine

Got A Crush On A Girl

♪

yea I got a crush on a girl
she works at the library
a true mother of pearl
maybe I'd marry

is she'd give me a whirl
I'll take her on a ferry
show her a world
that could pop a cherry

yea I got a crush on a a girl
yea yea
a crush on a girl
yea yea

come on baby
look me in the eye
smile back at me
and make me sigh

that smile you got
is so damn sweet
you get me so hot
from my head to my feet

yea I got a crush on a girl
yea yea
she's so damn pretty
yea yea
she doesn't live next door
yea yea
she lives in New York City
yea yea

if she'd give me a whirl
I'll take her on a ferry
show her a world
that could pop a cherry

yea I got a crush on a girl
yea yea
got a crush on a girl
yea yea

To Live

I was born
but do I live

I grew up
but did I give

I live in the USA
but can I choose
Yes I have a choice
win or lose
Its up to me
to be free

To fight
for that right

To vote
I have spoke

To participate
to congregate

Speak your mind
be kind

Cause words spoken
are a token

of my life
or your life

I live in the USA
but can I choose
Yes I have a choice
win or lose
Its up to me
to be free

Feeling Lucky

my left hand itches
lucky today I hope
on my way to the casino
what's my horoscope

lots of giveaways
hope there's one for me
lots of time to play
well we soon shall see

if the bells start to ring
and I begin to scream
if my machine sings
it's a winners dream

jackpot and moohlah
right up my alley
casino hoopla
no dilly dally

cause winning
is working
see me grinning
and smirking

I may be a sinner
soaking up the sun
yes I'm a winner
always having fun

Ridin'

The driving safety course, I took
Twice to be sure
Because I waited forty years to learn.

I passed the three day course
And in the end
My motorcycle license I did earn.

Now I ride my Yamaha
Down the road
Motor roaring like a lion.

I love to feel the wind
Whip my body
And feel like I am flyin'.

The next destination
Is yet
to be determined.

I just get on my bike
To see what next
Can be learned.

So ride again
I will
To see where life will lead.

And in the end
the wind
is the only fuel I need.

The Chase

what's that scratching noise
over my head
keeping me up
while lying in bed

my cats all about
chasing something
I'm freaking out
is it a wild thing

afraid to move
but hear a squeak
that's not a mouse
the tension peaks

arise I must
turning lights on
a showdow's found
on my curtain

a baby squirrel
not a mouse
that's what I found
loose in my house

the chase begins
cat squirrel and me
I hope I win
and set the squirrel free

I won I won
the ending is good
happy to say
I'm back sawing wood

Sick Who Me

sick who me
oh no not me
I'm too young
my songs not sung

sick who me
that can't be
please check again
again and again

sick who me
let's wait and see
I don't want to know
let's go to a show

sick who me
I just want to flee
I want an answer
but not cancer

sick who me
I'm going to the sea
where I can think
and unthink

Spring

riding along route 80
thinking just about
peering out the window
wanting just to shout

where are the green trees
I thought it was spring
not yet said the owl
leaves are just sprouting

the mountains will begin
to grow green again
in a few more weeks
just watch those peaks

for radiant beauty
and purple majesty
with the spring's rain
life blossoms again

turning brown to gold
from gold to green
the wonder of it all
one magnificent scene

Conflict

I don't want to argue
I don't want to fight
You only see it your way
so I can't make it right

not until you open your eyes
and see the light
that the one that loves you
would never take flight
but forced to I might

thinking about this dilemma
for many days and nights
trying to understand
this difficult plight

try as I may and
try as I might
I still can't seem
to make it right

without a fight
for what's right
do I call or wait some more
do I call or walk out the door

I don't want to argue
I don't want to fight
You only see it your way
so I can't make it right

Two Beach Chairs

Two beach chairs
on the sand
cuddling lovers
holding hands

gazing forward
toward infinity
as true love
is shared endlessly

Forever Friends

*Forever Friends
is a great thing
for forever
means no ending*

*I love you
I always will
and forever's
the word that
fits the bill*

*Thanks for the begining
and all to be in between
but the best part is forever
and what remains unseen*

*look forward to the future
with my forever friend
for there is comfort in knowing
this friendship has no end*